FIND YOUR

NATIONAL PARKS STAMPBOOK
FOR
KIDS

Attach an image of
yourself when starting
the book here!

This book belongs to:

_____

Age at start:_____

Date the adventure began:

_____

DEDICATION

This National Parks Notebook is dedicated to all the National Park Lovers out there who love to plan out and visit the state parks, and document their findings in the process.

You are my inspiration for producing books and I'm honored to be a part of keeping all of your notes and records organized.

How to use this National Parks Stamp Notebook:

This useful national parks project log book is a must-have for anyone that loves the art of travel and visiting the national state parks! You will love this easy to use journal to track and record all your national park activities.

Each interior page includes space to record & track the following:

Visit Date - Write down the date of the current park project.
Number of Days At The Park - Use this space to fill in the number of days you were theret.
Your Reflections On The Park - Record any thoughts, observations of this park.
Stamp or Sticker - Fill in the stamp or sticker in this space.

If you are new to the world of traveling to visit the national parks or have been at it for a while, this national park stamp book organizer is a must have! Can make a great useful gift for anyone that loves to visit the national state parks!

Have Fun!

reflection | noun | re·flec·tion

consideration of some subject matter, idea, or purpose

Take some time to reflect as you complete this book and your visit to the National Parks. Why are our National Parks important? What does this park, or this spot in the park mean to you? How will you help protect this park and our national resources?

Acadia National Park

Location: Maine
Year established: 1919
Visit Date:_____
Number of days at the park: _____
Your reflections on the park: _____
_____
_____
_____

Stamp Here

N.P. of American Samoa

Location: American Samoa

Year established: 1988

Visit Date:_____

Number of days at the park: _____

Your reflections on the park: _____

_____

_____

_____

Stamp Here

Arches National Park

Location: Utah

Year established: 1971

Visit Date:_____

Number of days at the park: _____

Your reflections on the park: _____

_____

_____

_____

Stamp Here

Badlands National Park

Location: South Dakota

Year established: 1978

Visit Date:_____

Number of days at the park: _____

Your reflections on the park: _____

_____

_____

_____

Stamp Here

Big Bend National Park

Location: Texas

Year established: 1974

Visit Date:_____

Number of days at the park: _____

Your reflections on the park: _____

_____

_____

_____

Stamp Here

Biscayne National Park

Location: Florida

Year established: 1980

Visit Date:_____

Number of days at the park: _____

Your reflections on the park: _____

_____

_____

_____

Stamp Here

Black Canyon - Gunnison

Location: Colorado

Year established: 1999

Visit Date:_____

Number of days at the park: _____

Your reflections on the park: _____

_____

_____

_____

Stamp Here

Bryce Canyon N.P

Location: Utah

Year established: 1928

Visit Date:_____

Number of days at the park: _____

Your reflections on the park: _____

_____

_____

_____

Stamp Here

Canyonlands N.P.

Location: Utah

Year established: 1964

Visit Date:_____

Number of days at the park: _____

Your reflections on the park: _____

_____

_____

_____

Stamp Here

Capital Reef N.P.

Location: Utah

Year established: 1971

Visit Date:_____

Number of days at the park: _____

Your reflections on the park: _____

_____

_____

_____

Stamp Here

Carlsbad Caverns N.P.

Location: New Mexico

Year established: 1930

Visit Date:_____

Number of days at the park: _____

Your reflections on the park: _____

_____

_____

_____

Stamp Here

Channel Islands N.P.

Location: California

Year established: 1980

Visit Date:_____

Number of days at the park: _____

Your reflections on the park: _____

_____

_____

_____

Stamp Here

Conagree National Park

Location: South Carolina

Year established: 2003

Visit Date:_____

Number of days at the park: _____

Your reflections on the park: _____

_____

_____

_____

Stamp Here

Crater Lake N.P.

Location: Oregon
Year established: 1902
Visit Date:_____
Number of days at the park: _____
Your reflections on the park: _____
_____
_____

_____

Stamp Here

Cuyahoga Valley N.P.

Location: Ohio
Year established: 2000
Visit Date:_____
Number of days at the park: _____
Your reflections on the park: _____
_____
_____
_____

Stamp Here

Death Valley N.P.

Location: California, Nevada
Year established: 1994
Visit Date:_____
Number of days at the park: _____
Your reflections on the park: _____
_____
_____
_____

Stamp Here

Denali National Park

Location: Alaska

Year established: 1917

Visit Date:_____

Number of days at the park: _____

Your reflections on the park: _____

_____

_____

_____

Stamp Here

Dry Tortugas N.P.

Location: Florida

Year established: 1992

Visit Date:_____

Number of days at the park: _____

Your reflections on the park: _____

_____

_____

_____

Stamp Here

Everglades N.P.

Location: Florida

Year established: 1934

Visit Date:_____

Number of days at the park: _____

Your reflections on the park: _____

_____

_____

_____

Stamp Here

Gates of the Arctic N.P.

Location: Alaska

Year established: 1980

Visit Date:_____

Number of days at the park: _____

Your reflections on the park: _____

_____

_____

_____

Stamp Here

Glacier National Park

Location: Montana
Year established: 1910
Visit Date:_____
Number of days at the park: _____
Your reflections on the park: _____
_____
_____
_____

Stamp Here

Glacier Bay N.P.

Location: Alaska
Year established: 1980
Visit Date:_____
Number of days at the park: _____
Your reflections on the park: _____
_____
_____
_____

Stamp Here

Grand Canyon N.P.

Location: Arizona

Year established: 1919

Visit Date:_____

Number of days at the park: _____

Your reflections on the park: _____

_____

_____

_____

Stamp Here

Grand Teton N.P.

Location: Wyoming

Year established: 1929

Visit Date:_____

Number of days at the park: _____

Your reflections on the park: _____

_____

_____

_____

Stamp Here

Great Basin N.P.

Location: Nevada
Year established: 1986
Visit Date:_____
Number of days at the park: _____
Your reflections on the park: _____
_____
_____
_____

Stamp Here

Great Sand Dunes N.P.

Location: Colorado

Year established: 2004

Visit Date:_____

Number of days at the park: _____

Your reflections on the park: _____

_____

_____

_____

Stamp Here

Great Smoky Mtns. N.P.

Location: Tennessee, North Carolina
Year established: 1934
Visit Date:_____
Number of days at the park: _____
Your reflections on the park: _____
_____
_____
_____

Stamp Here

Guadalupe N.P.

Location: Texas

Year established: 1966

Visit Date:_____

Number of days at the park: _____

Your reflections on the park: _____

_____

_____

_____

Stamp Here

Haleakalā National Park

Location: Hawai'i

Year established: 1916

Visit Date:_____

Number of days at the park: _____

Your reflections on the park: _____

_____

_____

_____

Stamp Here

Hawai'i Volcanoes N.P.

Location: Hawai'i
Year established: 1916
Visit Date:_____
Number of days at the park: _____
Your reflections on the park: _____
_____
_____
_____

Stamp Here

Hot Springs N.P.

Location: Arkansas

Year established: 1921

Visit Date:_____

Number of days at the park: _____

Your reflections on the park: _____

_____

_____

_____

Stamp Here

Isle Royale N.P.

Location: Michigan
Year established: 1940
Visit Date:_____
Number of days at the park: _____
Your reflections on the park: _____

_____

_____

_____

Stamp Here

Joshua Tree N.P.

Location: California

Year established: 1994

Visit Date:_____

Number of days at the park: _____

Your reflections on the park: _____

_____

_____

_____

Stamp Here

Katmai National Park

Location: Alaska

Year established: 1980

Visit Date:_____

Number of days at the park: _____

Your reflections on the park: _____

_____

_____

_____

Stamp Here

Kenai Fjords N.P.

Location: Alaska

Year established: 1980

Visit Date:_____

Number of days at the park: _____

Your reflections on the park: _____

_____

_____

_____

Stamp Here

Kings Canyon N.P.

Location: California

Year established: 1940

Visit Date:_____

Number of days at the park: _____

Your reflections on the park: _____

_____

_____

_____

Stamp Here

Kobuk Valley N.P.

Location: Alaska

Year established: 1980

Visit Date:_____

Number of days at the park: _____

Your reflections on the park: _____

_____

_____

_____

Stamp Here

Lake Clark N.P.

Location: Alaska

Year established: 1980

Visit Date:_____

Number of days at the park: _____

Your reflections on the park: _____

_____

_____

_____

Stamp Here

Lassen Volcanic N.P.

Location: California
Year established: 1916
Visit Date:_____
Number of days at the park: _____
Your reflections on the park: _____
_____
_____
_____

Stamp Here

Mammoth Cave N.P.

Location: Kentucky
Year established: 1941
Visit Date:_____
Number of days at the park: _____
Your reflections on the park: _____

_____
_____

_____

Stamp Here

Mesa Verde N.P.

Location: Colorado

Year established: 1906

Visit Date:_____

Number of days at the park: _____

Your reflections on the park: _____

_____

_____

_____

Stamp Here

Mount Rainier N.P.

Location: Washington

Year established: 1899

Visit Date:_____

Number of days at the park: _____

Your reflections on the park: _____

_____

_____

_____

Stamp Here

North Cascades N.P.

Location: Washington

Year established: 1968

Visit Date:_____

Number of days at the park: _____

Your reflections on the park: _____

_____

_____

_____

Stamp Here

Olympic National Park

Location: Washington
Year established: 1938
Visit Date:_____
Number of days at the park: _____
Your reflections on the park: _____
_____
_____
_____

Stamp Here

Petrified Forest N.P.

Location: Arizona

Year established: 1962

Visit Date:_____

Number of days at the park: _____

Your reflections on the park: _____

_____

_____

_____

Stamp Here

Pinnacles National Park

Location: California

Year established: 2013

Visit Date:_____

Number of days at the park: _____

Your reflections on the park: _____

_____

_____

_____

Stamp Here

Redwood National Park

Location: California

Year established: 1968

Visit Date:_____

Number of days at the park: _____

Your reflections on the park: _____

_____

_____

_____

Stamp Here

Rocky Mountain N.P.

Location: Colorado
Year established: 1915
Visit Date:_____
Number of days at the park: _____
Your reflections on the park: _____

_____

_____

_____

Stamp Here

Saguaro National Park

Location: Arizona

Year established: 1994

Visit Date:_____

Number of days at the park: _____

Your reflections on the park: _____

_____

_____

_____

Stamp Here

Sequoia National Park

Location: California

Year established: 1890

Visit Date:_____

Number of days at the park: _____

Your reflections on the park: _____

_____

_____

_____

Stamp Here

Shenandoah N.P.

Location: Virginia

Year established: 1935

Visit Date:_____

Number of days at the park: _____

Your reflections on the park: _____

_____

_____

_____

Stamp Here

Theodore Roosevelt N.P.

Location: North Dakota

Year established: 1978

Visit Date:_____

Number of days at the park: _____

Your reflections on the park: _____

_____

_____

_____

Stamp Here

Virgin Islands N.P.

Location: U.S. Virgin Islands
Year established: 1956
Visit Date:_____
Number of days at the park: _____
Your reflections on the park: _____
_____
_____
_____

Stamp Here

Voyageurs N.P.

Location: Minnesota

Year established: 1971

Visit Date:_____

Number of days at the park: _____

Your reflections on the park: _____

_____

_____

_____

Stamp Here

Wind Cave N.P.

Location: South Dakota

Year established: 1903

Visit Date:_____

Number of days at the park: _____

Your reflections on the park: _____

_____

_____

_____

Stamp Here

Wrangell–St. Elias N.P.

Location: Alaska
Year established: 1980
Visit Date:_____
Number of days at the park: _____
Your reflections on the park: _____
_____
_____
_____

Stamp Here

Yellowstone N.P.

Location: Wyoming, Montana, Idaho
Year established: 1872
Visit Date:_____
Number of days at the park: _____
Your reflections on the park: _____
_____
_____
_____

Stamp Here

Yosemite National Park

Location: California

Year established: 1890

Visit Date:_____

Number of days at the park: _____

Your reflections on the park: _____

_____

_____

_____

Stamp Here

Zion National Park

Location: Utah

Year established: 1919

Visit Date:_____

Number of days at the park: _____

Your reflections on the park: _____

_____

_____

_____

Stamp Here

Acadia National Park

Location: Maine

Year established: 1919

Visit Date:_____

Number of days at the park: _____

Your reflections on the park: _____

_____

_____

_____

Stamp Here

N.P. of American Samoa

Location: American Samoa

Year established: 1988

Visit Date:_____

Number of days at the park: _____

Your reflections on the park: _____

_____

_____

_____

Stamp Here

Arches National Park

Location: Utah

Year established: 1971

Visit Date:_____

Number of days at the park: _____

Your reflections on the park: _____

_____

_____

_____

Stamp Here

Badlands National Park

Location: South Dakota

Year established: 1978

Visit Date:_____

Number of days at the park: _____

Your reflections on the park: _____

_____

_____

_____

Stamp Here

Big Bend National Park

Location: Texas

Year established: 1974

Visit Date:_____

Number of days at the park: _____

Your reflections on the park: _____

_____

_____

_____

Stamp Here

Biscayne National Park

Location: Florida

Year established: 1980

Visit Date:_____

Number of days at the park: _____

Your reflections on the park: _____

_____

_____

_____

Stamp Here

Black Canyon - Gunnison

Location: Colorado

Year established: 1999

Visit Date:_____

Number of days at the park: _____

Your reflections on the park: _____

_____

_____

_____

Stamp Here

Bryce Canyon N.P

Location: Utah

Year established: 1928

Visit Date:_____

Number of days at the park: _____

Your reflections on the park: _____

_____

_____

_____

Stamp Here

Canyonlands N.P.

Location: Utah

Year established: 1964

Visit Date:_____

Number of days at the park: _____

Your reflections on the park: _____

_____

_____

_____

Capital Reef N.P.

Location: Utah

Year established: 1971

Visit Date:_____

Number of days at the park: _____

Your reflections on the park: _____

_____

_____

_____

Stamp Here

Carlsbad Caverns N.P.

Location: New Mexico

Year established: 1930

Visit Date:_____

Number of days at the park: _____

Your reflections on the park: _____

_____

_____

_____

Stamp Here

Channel Islands N.P.

Location: California

Year established: 1980

Visit Date:_____

Number of days at the park: _____

Your reflections on the park: _____

_____

_____

_____

Stamp Here

Conagree National Park

Location: South Carolina
Year established: 2003
Visit Date:_____
Number of days at the park: _____
Your reflections on the park: _____

_____

_____

_____

Stamp Here

Crater Lake N.P.

Location: Oregon

Year established: 1902

Visit Date:_____

Number of days at the park: _____

Your reflections on the park: _____

_____

_____

_____

Stamp Here

Cuyahoga Valley N.P.

Location: Ohio
Year established: 2000
Visit Date:_____
Number of days at the park: _____
Your reflections on the park: _____
_____
_____
_____

Stamp Here

Death Valley N.P.

Location: California, Nevada

Year established: 1994

Visit Date:_____

Number of days at the park: _____

Your reflections on the park: _____

_____

_____

_____

Stamp Here

Denali National Park

Location: Alaska

Year established: 1917

Visit Date:_____

Number of days at the park: _____

Your reflections on the park: _____

_____

_____

_____

Stamp Here

Dry Tortugas N.P.

Location: Florida

Year established: 1992

Visit Date:_____

Number of days at the park: _____

Your reflections on the park: _____

_____

_____

_____

Stamp Here

Everglades N.P.

Location: Florida

Year established: 1934

Visit Date:_____

Number of days at the park: _____

Your reflections on the park: _____

_____

_____

_____

Stamp Here

Gates of the Arctic N.P.

Location: Alaska

Year established: 1980

Visit Date:_____

Number of days at the park: _____

Your reflections on the park: _____

_____

_____

_____

Stamp Here

Glacier National Park

Location: Montana

Year established: 1910

Visit Date:_____

Number of days at the park: _____

Your reflections on the park: _____

_____

_____

_____

Stamp Here

Glacier Bay N.P.

Location: Alaska

Year established: 1980

Visit Date:_____

Number of days at the park: _____

Your reflections on the park: _____

_____

_____

_____

Stamp Here

Grand Canyon N.P.

Location: Arizona

Year established: 1919

Visit Date:_____

Number of days at the park: _____

Your reflections on the park: _____

_____

_____

_____

Stamp Here

Grand Teton N.P.

Location: Wyoming
Year established: 1929
Visit Date:_____
Number of days at the park: _____
Your reflections on the park: _____
_____
_____
_____

Stamp Here

Great Basin N.P.

Location: Nevada

Year established: 1986

Visit Date:_____

Number of days at the park: _____

Your reflections on the park: _____

_____

_____

_____

Stamp Here

Great Sand Dunes N.P.

Location: Colorado

Year established: 2004

Visit Date:_____

Number of days at the park: _____

Your reflections on the park: _____

_____

_____

_____

Stamp Here

Great Smoky Mtns. N.P.

Location: Tennessee, North Carolina

Year established: 1934

Visit Date:_____

Number of days at the park: _____

Your reflections on the park: _____

_____

_____

_____

Stamp Here

Guadalupe N.P.

Location: Texas

Year established: 1966

Visit Date:_____

Number of days at the park: _____

Your reflections on the park: _____

_____

_____

_____

Stamp Here

Haleakalā National Park

Location: Hawai'i
Year established: 1916
Visit Date:_____
Number of days at the park: _____
Your reflections on the park: _____
_____
_____
_____

Stamp Here

Hawai'i Volcanoes N.P.

Location: Hawai'i

Year established: 1916

Visit Date:_____

Number of days at the park: _____

Your reflections on the park: _____

_____

_____

_____

Stamp Here

Hot Springs N.P.

Location: Arkansas

Year established: 1921

Visit Date:_____

Number of days at the park: _____

Your reflections on the park: _____

_____

_____

_____

Stamp Here

Isle Royale N.P.

Location: Michigan
Year established: 1940
Visit Date:_____
Number of days at the park: _____
Your reflections on the park: _____
_____
_____
_____

Stamp Here

Joshua Tree N.P.

Location: California

Year established: 1994

Visit Date:_____

Number of days at the park: _____

Your reflections on the park: _____

_____

_____

_____

Stamp Here

Katmai National Park

Location: Alaska

Year established: 1980

Visit Date:_____

Number of days at the park: _____

Your reflections on the park: _____

_____

_____

_____

Stamp Here

Kenai Fjords N.P.

Location: Alaska

Year established: 1980

Visit Date:_____

Number of days at the park: _____

Your reflections on the park: _____

_____

_____

_____

Stamp Here

Kings Canyon N.P.

Location: California

Year established: 1940

Visit Date:_____

Number of days at the park: _____

Your reflections on the park: _____

_____

_____

_____

Stamp Here

Kobuk Valley N.P.

Location: Alaska

Year established: 1980

Visit Date:_____

Number of days at the park: _____

Your reflections on the park: _____

_____

_____

_____

Stamp Here

Lake Clark N.P.

Location: Alaska

Year established: 1980

Visit Date:_____

Number of days at the park: _____

Your reflections on the park: _____

_____

_____

_____

Stamp Here

Lassen Volcanic N.P.

Location: California

Year established: 1916

Visit Date:_____

Number of days at the park: _____

Your reflections on the park: _____

_____

_____

_____

Stamp Here

Mammoth Cave N.P.

Location: Kentucky
Year established: 1941
Visit Date:_____
Number of days at the park: _____
Your reflections on the park: _____
_____
_____
_____

Stamp Here

Mesa Verde N.P.

Location: Colorado
Year established: 1906
Visit Date:_____
Number of days at the park: _____
Your reflections on the park: _____
_____
_____
_____

Stamp Here

Mount Rainier N.P.

Location: Washington

Year established: 1899

Visit Date:_____

Number of days at the park: _____

Your reflections on the park: _____

_____

_____

_____

Stamp Here

North Cascades N.P.

Location: Washington
Year established: 1968
Visit Date:_____
Number of days at the park: _____
Your reflections on the park: _____

_____

_____

_____

Stamp Here

Olympic National Park

Location: Washington

Year established: 1938

Visit Date:_____

Number of days at the park: _____

Your reflections on the park: _____

_____

_____

_____

Stamp Here

Petrified Forest N.P.

Location: Arizona

Year established: 1962

Visit Date:_____

Number of days at the park: _____

Your reflections on the park: _____

_____

_____

_____

Stamp Here

Pinnacles National Park

Location: California

Year established: 2013

Visit Date:_____

Number of days at the park: _____

Your reflections on the park: _____

_____

_____

_____

Stamp Here